Original title:
Gingerbread Hearts and Christmas Stars

Copyright © 2024 Creative Arts Management OÜ
All rights reserved.

Author: Ophelia Ravenscroft
ISBN HARDBACK: 978-9916-90-852-5
ISBN PAPERBACK: 978-9916-90-853-2

Crafting Stars from Sweetness and Light

In the kitchen, flour flies,
Sugar dust like snowflakes rise,
Baking shapes that wink and cheer,
Whisking giggles, spreading cheer.

Silly molds that twist and turn,
Ovens hot, the candles burn,
Frosting smiles with candy eyes,
Each treat a tasty, sweet surprise.

The Joy of Giving with Sprinkles of Kindness

Boxes wrapped with bows on top,
Sweet delights, you just can't stop,
Sprinkles tumble, a colorful rain,
Deliver joy, let's bake again!

Neighbors grin with every bite,
Sharing goodies feels so right,
Laughter echoes through the bread,
Happiness, it's truly spread.

Memories Folded in Sweet Flour

Grandma's recipes laid out slow,
Rolling dreams into dough we throw,
A pinch of fun, a smile so bright,
Her stories mix with sugar's light.

When the oven's timer sings,
We'll dance like nuts on candy springs,
Tasting warmth from each delight,
Remembering joy in every bite.

Dances of Frost and Flavor

A waltz of icing on the plate,
Frosted trends that can't be late,
Chocolate dips and nutty sways,
Each cookie sends a shout and plays.

Lemon zest with a minty twist,
No one can resist this bliss,
Sweet concoctions in every jar,
Happiness baked like a shooting star.

Floury Whirls of Joyful Cheer

In the kitchen, flour flies,
Laughter dances, oh what a surprise!
Baking mishaps, giggles all around,
Sticky hands and joy abound.

Spatulas wave like tiny wands,
Pies and cakes made with our hands.
Sugar clouds and silly faces,
Cuisine chaos in all the places.

Sugar Stars that Light the Night

Sprinkled stars upon the floor,
Candy trails lead to the door.
Jellybean dreams like shooting stars,
A sugar rush from candy bars.

Frosting smiles with eyes so bright,
Cupcake towers reach new height.
Silly hats made from fruit loops,
Nibbling snacks in giggling troops.

A Pinch of Cinnamon and a Dash of Love

Cinnamon whispers in the air,
Tickling noses everywhere.
Cookies giggle from the rack,
Take a bite, and there's no lack.

Dancing spoons and joyful creaks,
Muffin tops, oh how they peek!
Mixing bowls and silly cheers,
Baking memories through the years.

Cookies Cradled by Starlight

Moonlit kitchens, cookies glow,
Chocolate chips in a sweet row.
Mice in aprons sneak a taste,
Racing hearts in all the haste.

Sugar sprinkles light the sky,
With every bite, a happy sigh.
All around, a tasty fray,
As laughter fills this sweet ballet.

Joyful Echoes Beneath the Snow

In the kitchen, flour flies,
Making shapes that catch your eyes.
The dough sings a happy tune,
As we dance beneath the moon.

Chubby angels, lopsided trees,
Making goodies with such ease.
Laughter spills like melted cheese,
Oh, the joy in every freeze!

Baking Delights and Starry Nights

Stirring batter, oh what fun,
Mixing sweet until we run!
Chasing sugar with a grin,
Shoveling goodies that make us spin.

With sprinkles flying through the air,
Our laughter echoes everywhere.
Christmas cheer in every bite,
Even burnt ones taste just right!

Echoes of Love in Oven's Glow

Rolling dough with flair and style,
Baking treats that make us smile.
Each cookie, much like a friend,
Brings us joy that will not end.

Cinnamon dreams and cocoa beams,
Life is sweeter than it seems.
We toast to cakes, our fruity flare,
A party's here; come everywhere!

Treasures Unearthed in Holiday Dough

In our aprons, we stand proud,
Whipping up a tasty crowd.
Hidden treasures wait inside,
Let's see what our spoons can hide.

Sprinkle laughter, pour on fun,
As our baking race's begun.
With each bite, a tale is spun,
A feast of giggles, everyone!

Whispers of Joy Beneath the Pine

In a kitchen filled with giggles,
The dough starts to dance and twirl,
Flour flies like snowflakes falling,
As we create our sugary world.

Sticky fingers, icing battles,
Sprinkles scattered far and wide,
Laughter echoes in the evening,
Where sweet dreams and fun collide.

Sugar Mementos of December's Embrace

Baking with a dash of mischief,
The mixer hums a jolly tune,
Mischief thrives in every corner,
While doughnuts hum beneath the moon.

With flour mustaches on our faces,
We shape each treat with little care,
Who knew that cookie dough could giggle,
And cheer us up with every flare?

Celestial Cookies and Candlelight Wishes

Candles flicker, shadows jive,
A cookie spaceship zooms on by,
Minty stars and cocoa comets,
With sprinkles dancing in the sky.

Each bite's a burst of holiday,
With flavors that could make you grin,
In this cookie-verse of laughter,
Where the fun is always a win!

A Canvas of Frost and Flavor

Frosting splatters, giggles fly,
Each cookie's adorned with flair,
A canvas painted with delight,
As we create our tasty wear.

With visions of desserts and laughter,
The oven beeps a merry tune,
We'll eat our way through cheeky dances,
In this festive kitchen boon.

Marvels Born from Spice and Kindness

In a kitchen bright, with flour in the air,
A chef wears a hat that's far too big to bear.
He dances 'round the counters, what a jolly sight,
Creating sweet delights that bring pure delight!

A pinch of love, a sprinkle of cheer,
His cookies giggle back, oh dear, oh dear!
One did a salsa, another a cha-cha,
They've got more moves than my Auntie Susha!

With frosting smiles and gumdrop eyes,
These baked little wonders reach for the skies.
But watch your step, they might start to roll,
Tumbling and laughing, they take on a stroll!

As warmth fills the air, the laughter proceeds,
He serves up joy, and his belly it feeds.
With sweets so funny, who could resist?
Beneath this spice, are hugs we can't miss!

Where Sugar Meets the Magic of Night

As nightfall whispers, twinkles abound,
The cookies plot mischief without making a sound.
They jump from the shelves, each one has a dream,
To twirl through the moonlight and dance by the stream!

With sparkly sprinkles that catch every gleam,
A cupcake hops past, oh what a team!
They giggle and wobble, in moonbeams they play,
Creating a riot in a sugary way!

A marshmallow bunny hops high with might,
While lollipops cheer from their fanciful flight.
They skip through the night, spreading giggles around,
In a world made of sweetness, where joy truly's found!

So when you feel blue, just peek at the stars,
Picture the sweets, those jubilant avatars.
In the shimmers of night, there's fun to declare,
With laughter and treats, love fills the air!

Glittering Echoes of Holiday Cheer

Baking with giggles, flour in the air,
Laughter erupts, we burst without care.
Chocolate chips flying, a sweet little fight,
We dance 'round the kitchen, hearts feeling light.

Sprinkles like confetti, on cookies we'll place,
Our messy creations, a sugar-fueled race.
Santa may chuckle, oh what a delight,
As we feast on our treats, all through the night.

Love Baked in the Warmth of Hearth

Mixing our wishes with batter and cream,
In a whirlwind of love, we frolic and beam.
The oven's our stage, with warmth we all glow,
As we craft lopsided sweets, putting on a show.

Merry tunes playing, we sing through the haze,
Pine-scented laughter fills all of our days.
With joy in each bite, we won't mind the mess,
We'll count every crumb as our sweet little bless.

Enchanted Evenings and Spiced Tales

A sprinkle of mischief, a dash of delight,
We gather our goodies, ready for the night.
With cookies so crumbled and icing askew,
We sit by the fire, while mischief brews.

Spicy tales swirling, we giggle and share,
Frosting-smeared faces and spritzed, tousled hair.
Under twinkling lights, we tumble and sip,
Each bite filled with laughter, our friendship, the tip.

Stars Beneath the Sugar Dust

With twinkling eyes, we sneak in a taste,
The joy of the season, oh, what a sweet waste!
Sugar-dusted dreams fall from our chins,
As giggles ignite beneath paper-thin skins.

Laughter like jingles dances all around,
The shape of our sweets, exquisitely round.
Stars twinkle bravely from each frosty edge,
As we toast to our wonders, all things we allege.

A Bake of Love Beneath the Pine

Flour flies like snowflakes bright,
As we whisk away our sweet delight.
Ovens hum with a joyful tune,
We dance around beneath the moon.

Sprinkles spill like tiny stars,
Sugar dough shaped into bizarre jars.
A ginger cat snags a rolling pin,
While laughter echoes, let the fun begin!

Sipping cocoa with marshmallow dreams,
Our kitchen sparks with laughter's beams.
Burning cookies – oh what a fate,
But who needs perfect when love's on a plate?

So gather round, let the laughter flow,
The mess we make is part of the show.
With every bite, a giggle or two,
For love is sweeter, just like our brew.

Frosted Dreams on Sugar Streets

Candy canes line the icy tracks,
Making sweets with silly hacks.
Frosty noses, cheeks aglow,
We trade our secrets on the go.

Whipped cream tops piled so high,
One big scoop — oh my, oh my!
Sugar sprinkles fall like rain,
While we giggle and hold our pain.

Bite-sized laughter, oh what a treat,
A giggle here, a stumble – now that's neat!
Slipping on frosting, a hilarious sight,
But festive chaos feels just right!

As twilight fades, we share our cheer,
Crafting momments that bring us near.
A sprinkle of joy as we take our seats,
In this sugary world with frosted feats.

Twinkling Lights and Spice-Kissed Delights

Twinkling bulbs dance on every tree,
Each shimmer whispers, 'Come play with me!'
Checking our stock of cookies and pies,
There's always room for one more surprise.

Sifting through laughs, with spice in the air,
A giggle mishap — oh, what a scare!
Cinnamon jokes that swirl and rise,
As we perfect our sweet-baking lies.

The oven's our sidekick, warm and embracing,
As sugar high leads to funny spacing.
Holiday spirit, a mess here and there,
Just proves that fun is worth the affair!

So lift your mug, make a cluttered cheer,
With laughter and love always near.
In a world where taste buds always reign,
We'll frolic in a spice-kissed domain.

Heartstrings Tied in Festive Ribbons

Ribbons tangled around the chairs,
As we dump sweet nothings everywhere.
Bow ties made of cookie dough,
Who knew baking could steal the show?

Laughter erupts, a whacky plan,
Gift-wrap pranks from our baking clan.
Cookies mixed with a dash of fun,
The night's not over, we've just begun!

Sprayed whipped cream, a cheeky delight,
Found on the face of brother's flight.
Pine-scented giggles fill the air,
As we dance around without a care.

So here's to the love and silly mess,
Wrapped in joy and playful excess.
With every bite that we concoct,
Together in laughter, our hearts will lock.

Frosty Hugs with a Dash of Spice

In the frosty air, we stand,
With cookies flying from my hand.
A sugar slip, a giggle shared,
As frost-kissed noses get ensnared.

Flour fights in a joyful spree,
Rolling dough like it's a bee.
With icing squiggles, laughter flows,
And ginger cheers in snowy bows.

Plates of Delight Under You

Beneath the tree, the sweet plates lie,
With candy canes that seem to fly.
I sneak a treat when no one sees,
Wondering why they taste like peas?

Friends gather round, we all collide,
With marshmallow snowmen, arms spread wide.
We munch our way through candy bliss,
And giggle when the cookies hiss.

The Aroma of Togetherness

The smell of spice fills every nook,
A fragrance fit for storybooks.
The oven sings a tune so sweet,
With playful bites that can't be beat.

Frosty mittens wave and sway,
As laughter scents the chilly day.
Each whiff of joy brings us near,
A playful dance, a festive cheer.

A Whisk of Imagination in a Chilly Romance

With a whisk in hand and dreams in mind,
We toss in giggles, see what we find.
A sprinkle here, a dash of flair,
Our snowy tales float through the air.

Mixing wishes like a potion,
With frosted joy and merry motion.
In the chill, we stir and glide,
A dance of laughter, side by side.

Under the Sugar Dust Sky

In a town of sweet delight,
Cookies dance in pure moonlight.
Frosting fights with candy canes,
Laughter echoes, sugar reigns.

Doughmen lose their heads in joy,
As kids run wild, oh what a ploy!
Spices sing in silly rhymes,
Tickling noses, passing times.

Snowflakes made of powdered bliss,
Chase the giggles, oh what a kiss!
Every moment, laughter flows,
As the sugary whirlwind grows.

With a wink and a smile so wide,
The jolly baker takes a ride.
On a sled made of candy dreams,
Life is sweeter than it seems.

A Symphony of Spice and Cheer

Baking songs fill every nook,
As spices dance in the old cookbook.
Nutmeg whispers, cinnamon sways,
A merry tune that always plays.

Doughnuts pirouette on the shelf,
Frosted smiles, oh, who needs help?
Sprinkles tumble like a cloudy show,
Every nibble brings high and low.

Laughter bubbles in rolling pins,
As mixers hum their silly sins.
Tasting spoons become great swords,
In this land of frosted fjords.

A cookie opera without a fuss,
Drama rises, they sing in a bus.
Join the feast, the jokes run free,
This symphony is plain to see.

Wishes Crafted with Love and Dough

In the kitchen mixes twirl,
Where every whisk will dance and whirl.
Flour flies like tiny snow,
While giggles weave through cookie dough.

Kid chefs don their sugar hats,
Crafting dreams and silly chats.
Rolling pins like magic wands,
Create each treat with clapping hands.

Joyful wishes baked in rows,
Every smile, a sweet expose.
With each bite, a sprinkle of luck,
In this oven, no room for yuck.

Sing along with floury tales,
As sweet nostalgia never fails.
With giggles echoing in the air,
Wishes rise, without a care.

Yuletide Nostalgia on Frosted Trails

Footprints made in icing snow,
Each step leads to places we know.
Gumdrop paths wind here and there,
Leading us to moments rare.

Carried by the scents of joy,
Each candy piece, a childhood toy.
With licorice sticks, we start to play,
On this sugary holiday.

Merry hiccups, laughter loud,
Underneath that frosty cloud.
With cookies lined in a row,
We trade our jokes, and giggles flow.

Gather 'round the dessert parade,
Where time slows down, and worries fade.
Let's race on this frosted trail,
With every heart's wish, we set sail.

A Tapestry Woven in Cookie Dreams

In a kitchen, all aglow,
Flour flies, and oh, what a show!
Cookies dancing on the floor,
Sugar rush, come back for more!

Merry laughter fills the air,
Frosting battles, who will dare?
Sprinkles land like tiny rain,
Each one adds to the sweet insane!

Rolling pins go round and round,
Crumbs and giggles all abound.
A doughnut's sigh, a cupcake's cheer,
Cooking chaos, but never fear!

With laughter baked into every bite,
We'll feast on cookie dreams tonight!
Grab a plate, let's start the fun,
This sugary journey has begun!

Cozy Fires and Sweet Reminders

By the fire, snug and tight,
Marshmallows roasting, what a sight!
Sippin' cocoa, feeling grand,
Watching as the sugar lands!

Bundled up in woolly threads,
Ginger snaps dance on our beds.
Tickling noses, warm with cheer,
Sugarplum visions drawing near!

A giggle pops with each warm sip,
Chocolate mustache on my lip.
S'mores and stories, oh what a tease,
Sharing laughter, such sweet ease!

The fire crackles, so divine,
With every bite, we sip and dine.
In this moment, all feels right,
Sweet reminders of this night!

Music of Sugar as Winter Falls

Snowflakes flutter, oh what joy,
Out comes the baker, oh my boy!
Pans all clatter, spoons and forks,
The sweet melody of holiday larks!

A dash of whimsy, a sprinkle of cheer,
Mixing up giggles, through the year.
Candy canes in a row they stand,
Winking at us, oh so grand!

Rascal rats in sugar hats,
Conversations 'bout pastry chats.
Sugar plums dance in the night,
While cookie soldiers prepare for flight!

Tinkling laughter fills the air,
Frosty face but we don't care.
In this banquet of delight,
Sugar's music makes it right!

Recipes Written in the Frost

Whispers of frost on the window pane,
Recipes dance in frosty rain.
Glazed carrots, silly and bold,
Telling stories yet untold!

Of marshmallow fluff and cookie dreams,
Lollipop forests bursting at the seams.
Ginger bears wear frosty coats,
As laughter bubbles in our throats!

A rolling pin races 'round the bend,
To sprinkle magic, not just pretend.
Frosty fingers dipped in fun,
Mixing joy until we're done!

In sweet chaos, we all belong,
The recipe writes its own song.
With every laugh, every bite,
Frosty tales of pure delight!

Sweet Pastries of Winter Nights

In the oven, dough does rise,
Sprinkled sugar, a sweet surprise.
Frosting battles on a plate,
Who will taste and who will wait?

Rolling pins on countertops,
Flour fights and silly flops.
Baking mishaps bring such glee,
Oops! That cookie's stuck on me!

Sprinkling spritz with all our might,
Chocolate drips that look just right.
With each bite, a flavor spree,
Dance with crumbs, oh, let it be!

Laughter echoes through the halls,
As icing drips and laughter calls.
Sweetened chaos, what a sight,
Winter fun, oh, what delight!

Twinkling Lights and Festive Delights

Twinkle lights on tangled wires,
Children dance by warming fires.
Eggnog spills, it paints the floor,
As we chase the pup for more!

Ornaments that play peek-a-boo,
On the tree, they're stuck like glue.
Garland woes, a tinsel mess,
Who knew festive could be such stress?

Table lays with treats galore,
Munching bites while we explore.
Fudge and cookies, all degrees,
Who ate the pie? Oh, not me, please!

Carols sung with silly cheer,
Off-key voices fill the year.
In this joy of frosty sights,
We find our fun in all the lights!

Frosted Dreams on Sugar Trails

Snowflakes swirl outside so bright,
While inside cookies take their flight.
Sugar rush from frosted dreams,
Giggles echo, or so it seems.

Rolling dough, we make a mess,
Sticky fingers, what a stress!
Spatulas up and whisks all whirl,
Merry madness, watch them twirl!

Chomping down on frosted treats,
Frosting face with sugary heats.
Who knew baking could be fun?
Wait until the night is done!

Glisten, sparkle, flour dusts fly,
S'mores erupt, oh my, oh my!
With each bite, there's joy and cheer,
Frosted giggles fill the sphere!

Shadows of Cinnamon in the Glow

In the corner, a pot does brew,
Cinnamon spice, a yummy hue.
Laughter rings as cookies sing,
Fluffy batter, let us bring!

Baking fails, they're tales so grand,
Behind the counter, dough in hand.
Puffed up biscuits laugh and tease,
"Can you catch me?" in the breeze!

Underneath the mistletoe,
Cocoa spills with friendly woe.
Marshmallow plops like snowball fights,
Winter giggles through the nights.

When the kitchen turns to glee,
Holiday magic sets us free.
With each bite, we laugh and toast,
To the treats we love the most!

Embers of Tradition in the Oven

In the kitchen where laughter thrives,
Flour flies and sugar dives.
Rolling pins twirl like a dance,
While sprinkles jump at every chance.

Grandma's recipe, a sacred scroll,
Kneading dough takes its toll.
Baking treats with giggles loud,
We're the silliest baking crowd!

The timer dings, it sings so sweet,
A crispy surprise, a sugary treat.
With a wink, we grab our trays,
It's festive chaos in so many ways!

Icing rivers, a stickiness spree,
Wielding spoons like swords, oh dear me!
We decorate with crooked glee,
These baked delights, proud as can be!

Crunchy Kisses and Icing Blessings

Sugar-coated whispers and sighs,
Our kitchen's filled with sugary spies.
Each batch brings a giggling cheer,
As frosting mustaches appear!

Chocolate chips in a sweet array,
Turn our frowns into play.
Grab your spoon, let's take a taste,
With tiny bites, we'll not waste!

Crunchy munches, a playful bite,
Giggling imps, oh what a sight!
Meringue kisses fly through the air,
With each one, we lose our hair!

A sprinkle fight breaks out, oh no!
In this doughy world, we share our glow.
With every laugh, our hearts align,
In this sweet chaos, we feel divine!

The Glow of Moonlit Bakers

Under the glow of the evening light,
We mix up mischief, oh what a sight.
Laughter blends with the scent of spice,
And the night seems remarkably nice!

Rolling dough like it's some game,
We're the bakers, and fun is our aim.
Sweet whispers and giggles bloom,
In our cozy, flour-filled room!

The echoes of laughter dance around,
As the dough gets squishy on the ground.
We sprinkle in joy with our hands so free,
This moonlit baking, pure glee!

Mixing flavors, we create a tale,
Of doughy dreams that never pale.
With tastes of joy, we fill our hearts,
In this merriment, the magic starts!

Heartfelt Tastes of a Spicy Wonderland

In a wonderland of flavor and fun,
We sprinkle cinnamon just for one.
Every bite a little surprise,
As we hide giggles behind our pies!

Merry moments baked with care,
Whisking wishes floating in the air.
With flavors dancing like a parade,
Oh, the joy that we've made!

Tasty bits on a crooked plate,
We laugh until it's getting late.
Gingerly tasting, we jump with flair,
What's this, a flour cloud in my hair?

In icing worlds where dreams ignite,
With every bite, we find delight.
Bakers full of spirit and cheer,
In this spicy land, let's stay right here!

Snowflakes Dancing on Cake Stands

Frosty flakes are falling down,
Landing soft on pastries round.
The baker sneezes, flour flies,
A powdery surprise arrives!

With laughing kids all in a race,
To grab a cookie, quick their pace.
But one gets stuck face-first in dough,
'Tis the season for a good show!

Sprinkles scattered like confetti,
Silly grins are looking steady.
As icicles, they try to skate,
On plates of sweets, oh what a fate!

So let us feast, dance, and munch,
With joyful giggles and a crunch.
For every bite brings pure delight,
In the sweet chaos of the night!

Cookies of Memory and Soft Laughter

A rolling pin goes whack and thump,
As flour flies, we start to jump.
Mismatched sprinkles, crooked designs,
We laugh till biscuits blur the lines!

Oh, Auntie's secret recipe,
Has vanished! Now, what could it be?
A dash of this, a smidge of that,
And flour dust on the dog's fat.

Grandpa's dance while icing flows,
With frosting beards and ticklish toes.
As giggles echo from every nook,
Each cookie's baked with love, not a book!

When friends arrive, we share a bite,
A table full, what a sight!
With cookies stacked to the very top,
We munch and laugh, we just won't stop!

Festive Whirls Beneath Copper Skies

The sky's alive with twinkling lights,
While elves spin tales of wondrous nights.
In copper hues, we dance and play,
As cookies crumble and children sway!

With merry tunes, our hearts will sing,
As laughter bounces like a spring.
Lemon zest and chocolate streams,
Tickling noses, igniting dreams!

A pie chart of flavors, round and bright,
A mishap here, a frosty flight.
With every bite, a new surprise,
As ginger snaps dance before our eyes!

So raise your mugs to all that's sweet,
In copper skies, there's nothing quite neat.
As love and laughter stir the air,
Together we feast without a care!

Warmth in Every Baked Delight

From the oven comes a fragrant wave,
We dive in quick, dessert we crave.
Each warm bite, a chuckle shared,
Chocolate chunks and smiles prepared!

Cookies stacked like little towers,
We devour them in festive hours.
With every crumb, silliness grows,
As flour fights become our show!

A sprinkle here, and frosting there,
Creating cookies that wouldn't dare.
They giggle back, with icing smiles,
"Merry munching!" spans the miles!

So join this feast, you won't regret,
With pots of laughter, no room for fret.
In every bake, there's love and mirth,
A joyful reminder of our worth!

Frosty Kisses and Recipe Secrets

In the kitchen, flour flies,
Cookies dance beneath the skies.
A pinch of laughter, sugar spry,
Watch the frosting, oh my my!

Whisking dreams in bowls so wide,
I wore icing like a guide.
Sprinkles raining, a sweet parade,
Who knew baking could be played?

My cat, he jumps for a taste,
While I scramble, in a haste.
With chocolate chips like scattered stars,
We laugh so hard, forget our scars.

Frosting fights, and sticky hands,
Giggling softly, close we stand.
Each creation, a joyful tease,
In our feast of silly peace.

A Journey through Spice and Starlight

In a pot, a mystery brews,
Sipping cider, we chase our blues.
Nutmeg giggles, cinnamon grins,
Oh the fun when the baking begins!

Racing to catch the runaway spoon,
Doughnuts spinning, dancing 'til June.
Pumpkin hats on our heads sit tight,
Who knew cooking could be such a fright?

Mixing flavors, a wild affair,
Flour dust settles in the air.
We twirl and spin, let laughter soar,
With each batch, we want more and more!

Under twinkling lights, we play,
A pinch of this, a dash of gay.
In our kitchen, all things bright,
Spice and joy, a silly sight!

Melodies of Milk and Mirth

Milk mustaches, a charming sight,
Sipping cocoa, hearts take flight.
Whisking giggles, splash of foam,
In this kitchen, we feel at home.

Cookies stacked like little dreams,
Syrups drip in sweetened streams.
Chasing crumbs with joyful squeals,
Life is grand with laughter's wheels!

Songs of whiskers, karaoke fun,
Baking battles, who's next to run?
Celestial sprinkles on every batch,
Oh the joys we love to catch!

We twirl around, a playful scene,
In this chaos, we feel like queens.
Melodies sweet, let friendships grow,
With each cookie, love we sow.

Crumbs of Kindness on Snowy Paths

On snowy streets, we leave a trail,
Crumbs of kindness, will they prevail?
Giggles echo in winter's air,
A sprinkle of cheer, everywhere!

Snowball fights end in yummy treats,
Chocolate shouts from happy fleets.
Sleighs down hills, hearts racing fast,
Who knew kindness would ever last?

Muffin tops and berry pies,
Laughter twinkling in our eyes.
Each recipe holds a friendship's bliss,
In this season, we can't miss!

Candied laughter, a cozy cheer,
Baking moments, we hold dear.
On snowy paths, our hearts renew,
With every crumb, a love so true.

Glimmers of Hope in Every Confection

In the kitchen, chaos reigns,
Flour's flying like snowflakes.
Mittens on, I make strange gains,
Baking treats that giggle and shake.

Sugar sprites dance in a bowl,
Chanting songs of sweet delight.
I mix and brew without control,
A laughter storm in full flight.

Choco chips roll like tumbleweeds,
Marshmallow snowmen start to form.
Each little treat fulfills my needs,
A tasty twist in festive norm.

When cookies smile, they bring such cheer,
Joy is served with sprinkles bright.
No room for doubt, just bake the gear,
And load my plate with pure delight.

Twinkling Frosting on Whimsy Wings

Frosting glimmers like a star,
Piping bags become my wand.
Sugar blooms from near and far,
As I create a pastry pond.

With every swirl, a giggle spills,
Colorful chaos on the plate.
Each cupcake crowned with sweet frills,
Whimsical dreams that taste so great.

Candy canes form a merry crew,
They march on frosting roads so wide.
Jellybeans in gumdrop hue,
Play hide and seek, they won't abide.

The icing shines, a playful tune,
With every bite, I burst with glee.
Frozen laughter in the noon,
Sugar magic's all I see.

Echoes of Laughter in a Winter Wonderland

Snowflakes dance on frosted roofs,
While cookies giggle, oh so round.
Peppermint sticks play silly hooves,
In a world where joy is found.

Caramel rivers overflow,
Sledding rides with candy teams.
Chubby snowmen steal the show,
In a land of sugary dreams.

Marzipan critters prance and play,
Whipped cream clouds float all around.
Every munch brings out the sway,
In this laughter-filled snowy ground.

Gifts of giggles all abound,
With each bite, I cheer and sing.
In this wonderland, I've found,
Delight that makes my heart take wing.

The Magic of Flavor and Light

In the oven, magic starts,
Bubbling joy, a rising scent.
With every bite, it warms our hearts,
Sprinkled dreams that won't relent.

Syrupy trails of treasure flow,
Encircling smiles again and again.
Bright colors dance, a delicious show,
Recalling moments that end in zen.

Lemon zings and berry kicks,
They join together in perfect match.
The pan is filled with quirky tricks,
As flavors bubble and hatch.

So gather 'round the tastiest treat,
With giggles adding to the fun.
In every flavor, joy we meet,
Underneath the warming sun.

Echoes of Laughter in Frosty Patterns

Snowflakes tumble, oh what a sight,
A snowman's hat, crooked but bright.
Laughter echoes through crisp, cold air,
As snowballs fly without a care.

Kittens chase shadows, pouncing with glee,
While clumsy dogs bark at the tree.
Frosty peeks out, his nose turns red,
To the snowball fight going on in his head.

Cookies turn brown, the timer beeps,
The cat stares at treats, then quietly creeps.
A ginger snap jumps straight from the shelf,
"Did you see that?" gasps an elf to himself!

Chill a fizzy drink, add one funny hat,
The celebration gets loud, oh imagine that!
With giggles and cheers, the night carries on,
Until the frost fades with the coming dawn.

The Night's Sweet Serenade

Bells jingle softly, a melody sweet,
With ribbons and laughter, it's quite the treat.
Cookies on plates, just out of reach,
In kitchens, there's chaos, a funny speech.

Squeaky toys sing, in a playful tune,
As baby's first taste of warm marzipan moon.
Frothy warm drinks spill over the side,
While uncle spills eggnog and runs to hide!

Decked halls glimmer, a glitter-filled brawl,
With ornaments bouncing, oh they're bound to fall.
Candles flicker, telling tales with a grin;
Ginger can't dance, yet he tries to spin!

Under the mistletoe, what might occur?
A grandma with cookies, a giggle and stir.
As sugar plums laugh in the evening glow,
This night's serenade steals the show!

Love Letters in Vanilla Hues

Whispers of frosting, sweet letters sent,
Find joy in the batter, a crumbly event.
With sprinkles and giggles, the kitchen's alive,
As flour explosions ensure we all thrive.

Peeking at notes tucked in each treat,
All jokes and puns, they're ludicrously sweet.
Couches invite us, let's lounge and chew,
As friends share secrets aflame with the brew.

Candied old secrets, they dance on our lips,
While children plot schemes for some sneaky quick nibbles.
Laughter erupts like a stirring spoon swirls,
You can't spell "holiday" without giggles and twirls!

With icing galore, these love notes take flight,
Each bite feels joyous, oh what a delight!
Loving the mayhem, we cheer and we sing,
Enjoying this banquet that shenanigans bring!

Hearts that Dance with Holiday Cheer

Oh look at that waltz, with a skip and a hop,
At the holiday party, we can't seem to stop.
With sugarplum fairies twirling like hats,
As Gramps busts a move, while the dog chases cats.

Tinsel's a twister, all tangled in curls,
While aunties sip cider, their laughter unfurls.
Hats made of holly, and boots laced with glee,
Dance floors erupt to a jolly decree!

Popcorn cascades from a garland gone wild,
Sprightly decor, like a sugar-fueled child.
Friends share their quirks with exaggerated flair,
While snowflakes giggle, floating high in the air.

So let's raise our glasses, toast to the fun,
With wishes for laughter, as bright as the sun.
Hearts that keep dancing, in joy and in cheer,
Together we bring the holiday near!

The Flavor of Holiday Wishes

In the kitchen, a dough ball spins,
Sugar plums dance, oh where to begin?
Rolling pins flying, frosting takes flight,
Tasting the chaos, what a delight!

Neighbors peek in with curious grins,
Catching the scent as the laughter begins.
Whisking our dreams with flour on nose,
Peculiar concoctions, nobody knows!

Eggnog spills down, a slippery floor,
Tiny reindeer plotting, oh what a chore!
Candy canes dangling, a vibrant display,
As we mix up trouble, come join in the play!

Gifts wrapped in sparkles, all tied with a bow,
Under the tree, we sneak in a throw.
With smiles and giggles, our holiday sway,
Creating sweet flavors that brighten the day!

Sugar Coated Memories Under the Mistletoe

In the corner, old cookies start to smirk,
Wondering who will do the silly jerk?
Under the sprigs, laughter erupts wide,
With sugar-coated giggles, teamwork applied!

The cat in a sweater looks quite absurd,
Chasing a candy cane like it's a bird.
Kittens and cookies, a comical sight,
With mischief around, how could it not bite?

We raise our cups filled with peppermint cheer,
While stories of past years bring nostalgia near.
Hot cocoa spills over, a marshmallow sea,
Sipping on laughter, I'm glad you're with me!

Under bright lights that twinkle in glee,
We toast to the wonders that are yet to be.
With sugar swirling, the joy carries on,
Memories crafted until the dawn!

Candlelit Secrets in the Frost

Beneath the glow of candles ablaze,
Whispers of wonders fill frosty displays.
Snowflakes giggle as they tickle my nose,
Dreaming of sweetness where laughter flows.

Wrapped in soft blankets, we sip and we chat,
Building our fort like a family of rats.
Snowmen stand guard with their carrot nose,
As we share our secrets where no one knows!

Cinnamon dances in the evening air,
Eggnog mustache, oh my, don't you dare!
Tickling the noggin with sprinkles galore,
Candlelit mysteries we can't help but score.

Outside a snowball fight bids hello,
While inside we scramble for cocoa to flow.
With giggles and warmth from our cozy nest,
This festive season's the very best!

Crumbs of Joy in the Warmth

In the oven, a batch of fun is a-brewing,
Butter and sugar, everyone's chewing.
Sneaky little bites, we're all having fun,
Crumbs of joy brimming, we've only begun!

Silly hats crafted with marshmallow fluff,
Laughing so loud, can never get enough!
A parade of cookies, each one a star,
Baking adventures, oh look, there's a car!

Wintery wonders breathe magic tonight,
Giggling children in pajamas so tight.
Flakes swirl outside while we dance around,
In the warmth of the kitchen, our joy is profound!

So raise up your mugs, let laughter unfold,
With sweet little treats, more precious than gold.
Wrapped in the spirit of festive delight,
We savor the moments, from morning till night!

Celestial Whispers on Iced Wings

In a kitchen of wonders, flour flies,
Sugar sprinkles like snow from the skies.
With each pop of dough and roll of a pin,
Laughter echoes, let the shenanigans begin.

A star-shaped cookie with a mischievous grin,
Slips from the counter, oh where has it been?
Chasing it down, the dog starts to prance,
While we giggle and trip, immersed in the dance.

Candies collide in a colorful storm,
Frosting smiles, oh, it keeps us warm.
With a dash of chaos, joy's in the mix,
As we nibble on sweets, unstoppable tricks.

Under the twinkle of bright fairy lights,
We craft our delights on those chilly nights.
A confectionery mess, but we wouldn't replace,
The joy of our laughter, that sweet, silly chase.

A Festival of Sweets Amidst the Stars

The moon winks softly, a playful delight,
While chocolate drops tumble, a sugary sight.
With gumdrop mountains and jellybean skies,
Who knew that candy could be so wise?

Cookies parade with icing galore,
Each taking a bow, then bursting in roar.
A lollipop jester, it spins and it twirls,
Joining the fun with a dance of swirls.

The stars burst with laughter, glowing so bright,
As cookies and candies join in the flight.
A sprinkle of chaos, frosting all around,
In this sweet orchestra, pure joy can be found.

Laughter erupts when we bite into cake,
The frosting explodes, oh, what a mistake!
Yet with giggles and grins, who cares about mess?
In this festival of sweets, we simply feel blessed.

Nostalgia Wrapped in Sugar Coating.

A whiff of vanilla brings back the cheer,
Of childhood giggles, the magic is near.
With every sweet bite of the treats we made,
Memories wrapped in a sugary cascade.

Oh, the chaos of sprinkles, paths of delight,
As flour dust clouds settle, our hearts take flight.
With stories of mischief, flour on our nose,
In this sweet nostalgia, laughter just flows.

Raspberry jam hugs between soft, warm bread,
While chocolate surprises float in our head.
Taste buds awaken to flavors so bold,
Each bite brings a tale of excitement retold.

As we reminisce in our sugar-coated gowns,
Like clowns in the kitchen, we wear frosting crowns.
With each sweet creation that looks less than fine,
We feast on our laughter, it's truly divine!

Sweet Whispers of Winter Nights

In the chill of the night, a whisper so sweet,
As cookie dough dances to a playful beat.
Cinnamon swirls with a giggle and shout,
Creating a ruckus, we're never in doubt.

Little marshmallow stars float in our mugs,
While stubborn candy canes pull us like tugs.
Each sticky endeavor, a sweet little jest,
In this winter chaos, we truly are blessed.

Ginger-spiced giggles fill up the room,
As frosting escapes like a startled balloon.
Sprinkles sprinkle the air, confetti of fun,
December's mischief, second to none.

With laughter as bright as the lights on the tree,
Each sugary moment as sweet as can be.
In the glow of the kitchen, our hearts all ignite,
In these winter nights, everything feels right.

Stars Adrift on a Winter's Path

In the kitchen, flour flies with cheer,
Cookies dance, spreading joy so near.
Chocolates giggle, hiding in their wraps,
Sweet surprises make the best of naps.

A snowman sneezes, puffing out his nose,
As marshmallows tumble, in fluffy clothes.
Giggles echo as the dough takes flight,
Who knew baking could be such delight?

With each doughy heart and playful grin,
The laughter rises, let the fun begin!
Rolling pins spin like tops in a show,
Who knew sugar could sparkle and glow?

Under twinkling lights, all the treats do play,
They waltz and jiggle, keeping blues away.
With each little bite, a giggle ignites,
Stars above watch this merry, sweet sight.

Tender Moments in Icing Dreams

Frosting rivers run down cookie hills,
With sprinkles that tickle and sweet candy thrills.
Gummies are whispering secrets so grand,
In this sugary world, where giggles expand.

A tiny elf snickers, sneaking some bites,
While sugarplums prance in their bold winter tights.
With icing as glimmer, they craft a fine cheer,
In the land of sweet dreams, no room for a tear.

Giggles burst forth from the warm oven door,
As the smelly scent of spice starts to pour.
In this magical kitchen, mess is a game,
With winkles of laughter, we all play the same.

In the heart of October, we craft for the feast,
With bowls overflowing, the joy won't cease.
Sugar miracles rise, please don't let them sink,
In these icing dreams, let's all share a wink.

Warm Hugs in a Flour Dust Dance

With laughter and giggles, we roll out the dough,
A whirlwind of flour puts on quite a show.
Cookies in pajamas, sweet chaos abounds,
A dance of the bakers, where silliness sounds.

Cinnamon swirls and a dash of surprise,
As ginger snaps giggle, oh what a rise!
Sprinkling joy, we twirl with delight,
Who knew baking could feel so bright?

With spatulas twirling in a joyous spree,
We mix, we knead, stopping for tea.
As the oven hums a comforting tune,
If cookies could sing, oh, how they'd croon!

In the warm glow of the kitchen's soft light,
We sprinkle the night, and our hearts take flight.
With hugs made of laughter, the sweetest of dances,
In the world of baked dreams, happiness prances.

A Sprinkle of Wonder and Joy

A dash of delight in each sugary bite,
With glee and with laughter, the treats take flight.
Dancing and twirling, the candies do sing,
As whistles of joy in the oven take wing.

A rush of excitement fills every nook,
As cookies tell tales from the heart of the book.
With pockets of frosting and jelly so red,
The robots in aprons are earning their bread.

What if marshmallows could talk and be wise?
They'd chuckle and banter with stars in their eyes.
In the giggly kitchen where happiness dwells,
We sprinkle our laughter, and all is a spell.

When sugar unites, we've got a big win,
With hugs made of laughter, let the magic begin.
So join in the fun with a smile and a cheer,
For every sweet moment gives joy to the year.

The Night of Tasteful Wishes

On a snowy eve, we gather round,
With cookies stacked, oh what a mound!
Dreams of frosting dance in the air,
As we munch with giggles, without a care.

Sprinkles like confetti, bright and bold,
Tales of mishaps warmly retold.
A cookie crumbles, laughter erupts,
And suddenly, we're all little pups!

Sweet treats in hand, we raise our cheers,
To stories of burnt pies and childhood fears.
With each sugary bite, the joy just swells,
In this wacky night, who needs fancy bells?

As the moon shines down on our festive spree,
We cherish these moments, wild and free.
In the land of laughter, we'll always find,
A slice of happiness, perfectly designed.

Laughter Laced in Sugar and Spice

A dash of giggles, a sprinkle of fun,
In the kitchen chaos, a race to be done.
Burnt edges crying, not quite the goal,
Yet laughter rings louder than the cookie's role.

Mixing and stirring, oh what a sight,
Ginger in hand, we bake through the night.
Cookies that wobble, like my stubborn cat,
Each bite is a joy, imagine that!

Frosting fingers and every plate cleared,
We wear our dessert like a badge, revered.
Chocolate smears and powdered delight,
With giggles that sparkle, the perfect night.

As we cozy up with our sugar high,
We know it's the laughter that makes us fly.
In this sweet wonder, we'll always rhyme,
With every sweet moment, we cherish our time.

Hands that Craft with Love

With flour on fingers, we start the show,
Rolling and cutting, oh look at it grow!
Star shapes and hearts, what will they be?
A masterpiece crafted, just wait and see!

The oven's warm glow, a beckoning light,
As we dance round the kitchen, hearts feeling bright.
Sticky embraces, dough on our face,
In this sweet workshop, we find our place.

Some cookies go missing—are they for me?
A nibble confirmed just brings such glee.
We giggle at crumbs that cover the floor,
A delicious disaster, who could want more?

As the treats cool down with a whimsical flair,
Our hearts are the magic we all love to share.
With icing and laughter, we craft our delight,
This cozy creation feels so very right.

Warmth Wrapped in Sweet Memories

Under twinkling lights, we gather as one,
With tales of mishaps, and laughter begun.
Cookies adorned with a colorful kiss,
Bring smiles and warmth, oh, what bliss!

With family around, the joy multiplies,
As mischief unfolds, and the laughter flies.
A missing cookie, was it me who ate?
In joyfully scandalous moments, we're fate!

A sprinkle of joy, on this winter's eve,
As we sip hot cocoa, it's hard to believe.
That memories wrapped in sweet little bites,
Create stories and laughter on chilly nights.

So here's to the fun in this festive spread,
Where smiles grow larger with ice cream as thread.
In hugs and delights, we know we will find,
The sweetest of treasures are those intertwined.

Hearthside Laughter and Frosty Breezes

The oven hums a merry tune,
Cookies dance like they're on the moon.
Chubby cheeks with frosting smeared,
Silent night? Not when we've cheered!

Snowflakes tumble through the air,
As we toss flour without a care.
Grandpa's dreaming of a treat,
But we'll save him stale old beet!

Reflections of Joy in Icing Dreams

A sprinkle here, a dash of cheer,
A gummy bear, oh my, we steer!
With sticky hands and laughing souls,
We craft delight in scrumptious roles.

The cocoa spills, the marshmallows fly,
Mom's on the phone – it's a baking lie!
We claim our world with icing flair,
And hide the evidence everywhere!

Candlelit Moments and Sweet Hues

With candle glow, we jive and jig,
A chocolate tree? It's not too big!
The cat snags a pastry rush,
While we giggle, oh what a crush!

Laughter rings like chiming bells,
Who knew baking could be such spells?
In sugar rush we take our flight,
With cookie castles built tonight!

A Tapestry of Flavor and Wonder

The sprinkles twirl like tiny stars,
We'll dress the pastry with chocolate bars!
A tug, a pull, then flour in hair,
Oh what fun, but do we dare?

Our chocolate stash disappears fast,
While giggling at the frosty blast.
A taste of chaos, joy entwined,
This festive frenzy's one of a kind!

Festive Whirls in a Cozy Kitchen

In a kitchen filled with laughter, mistletoe swings,
The dog in a Santa hat, oh, the joy it brings.
Flour flies in a flurry, a snowstorm of fun,
We roll out the dough, and the chaos has begun.

Cinnamon giggles and nutmeg sneezes,
Silly faces and doughy wheezes.
Cookie cutters dance like they're having a ball,
Watch out for the frosting—it's a sweet free-for-all!

The oven's a monster, growling away,
Chasing the cookie thieves who dare to stray.
On a plate shines a creation, oddly shaped and bright,
Is that a bear or a reindeer? What a funny sight!

Finally, we feast on our crafty display,
With sprinkles on each one, we munch and we sway.
Laughter fills the room, joyfully we shout,
Next year, more chaos—there's no doubt!

The Heart of Celebration Unleashed

A jolly old elf with a belly so round,
Sneaks by the window without making a sound.
With twinkling eyes, he dips his big spoon,
In a pot of hot cocoa beneath the full moon.

The children conspire, with chocolate in hand,
As sugar dust fairies frolic and stand.
Snickerdoodles giggle, they've lost track of time,
When one falls off the counter—oh, such a crime!

Marshmallows bounce like little fluffy sheep,
In festive hot drinks where secrets can creep.
Everyone smiles, listed on Santa's nice page,
While a cat in a hoodie is ready to stage.

At the heart of this hullabaloo, chimes a cheer,
With friends gathered close, all filled with good cheer.
Let's dance in the kitchen, our hearts all aglow,
Next year's recipe? Here, just go with the flow!

Edible Joys in a Frosty Wonderland

In a white wonderland where the ginger snaps run,
Marshmallow snowmen bask under the sun.
With candies for buttons and smiles made of gum,
Who knew holiday snacks could be this much fun?

Icicles hanging like sweet syrup boots,
While rogue peppermint sticks plot sneaky pursuits.
The sleds are all cookies, and the hills made of cake,
Sledding down laughter, oh what fun we can make!

Frosting like paint on a crispy blank slate,
Fondant adventures await on each plate.
With sprinkles like stars scattered near and far,
A festive parade, an edible bazaar!

As giggles erupt over cocoa spills,
We munch on our crafts while sharing the thrills.
With each festive bite, our spirits take flight,
In this frosty wonderland, everything's right!

Sprinkling Hope on a Chilly Day

When the chill of December wraps round like a hug,
We gather around to craft sweets with a shrug.
With the roll of the dough and a sprinkle of cheer,
Laughter erupts as the pastries appear.

Silly slogans on icing get drawn, oh so bright,
"Eat me, I'm tasty!" in such comical spite.
Snowflakes in sugar arrange quite the show,
While one baker sneezes, and frosting will go!

Chattering ginger figures hold court on the floor,
With gummy bear guards standing watch at the door.
The oven, our dragon, hums tunes with delight,
Creating a feast that shines through the night.

We gather together with families and friends,
As the laughter and joy of the season transcends.
With sprinkles of hope in each dish that we bake,
On this chilly day, many memories we make!

Milton Keynes UK
Ingram Content Group UK Ltd.
UKHW021628011224
451755UK00010B/506